In My
Upstairs
Room

In My Upstairs Room

Daily Thoughts About Answered Prayer

MAB GRAFF HOOVER

ZONDERVAN
PUBLISHING HOUSE

OF THE ZONDERVAN CORPORATION | GRAND RAPIDS MICHIGAN 49506

In My Upstairs Room
Copyright © 1982 by The Zondervan Corporation
Grand Rapids, Michigan

Library of Congress Cataloging in Publication Data

Hoover, Mab Graff.
    In my upstairs room.

    1. Christian life—1960– 2. Hoover, Mab Graff. I. Title.
BV4501.2.H584   1982   209'.2'4 [B]   82-11186
ISBN 0-310-35632-6

Edited by Evelyn Bence
Designed by John Iwema

Except for the author's immediate family, all names have been changed. All answers to prayer are real, and either happened to the author or to someone she has known.

Scripture quotations, unless otherwise noted, are taken from the New International Version of the Bible, copyright© 1978 by the New York International Bible Society.

Printed in the United States of America

83 84 85 86 87 88 — 9 8 7 6 5 4 3 2

Contents

Preface   7
Losses and Gains   11
Mosquito Mastered   13
Yours for the Asking   15
Never Too Late   17
Passing the Plate   19
Giving Gifts   21
Heartache   23
Old Flames   25
Following the Leader   27
Good News!   29
Both Feet on the Ground   31
Okay? Okay. Okay!   33
Opposing Forces   35
My Jerusalem   37
To Whom Am I Speaking?   39
The Eyes Have It   41
Match Breaker?   43
Deep and Wide   45
Oh Yes! Maybe!   47
Things Not Seen   49
Mind Sets   51
Green Lights   53
The Disaster in My Mind   55
Minimum Payments   57
The Satin Finish   59
A Change of Heart   61

A Battle Call   63
What Can I Say?   65
Red-letter Lesson   67
The Turned Table   69
Out of Control   71
When the Heat Is On   73
The Mailman Cometh   75
He Is Life!   77
Show Me!   79
Waiting for Weight   81
Bygones   83
Mirror, Mirror, on the Wall   85
A Time for Us?   87

Preface

Prayer has been an important part of my life ever since I became a Christian. But there have been times when the Lord seemed to underscore how important prayer is.

The Lord used a conversation with a young man I was working with to teach me a lot about prayer.

This fellow was a school teacher and part-time draftsman. My husband, who was in business for himself as a contractor, had hired him for the summer, and since I was bookkeeper and secretary in the same office, we saw each other every day. We were both Christians and often talked about spiritual things. One day we got on the subject of prayer.

"I don't pray for things to happen," he said. "I used to. But, God is sovereign. He already has everything planned, so why pray? I just thank Him for whatever He is going to do."

We discussed this for a while, and I became flustered.

"How about Hezekiah?" I asked. "He asked God to spare his life, and God gave him fifteen more years to live!"

His eyes twinkled. "Yes, but don't you see? It was already planned that he'd have a longer life."

"But what if Hezekiah hadn't asked?"

"God knew he would ask!"

At this point we stopped arguing. I rebelled inside at what he said, yet I, too, believed the Lord knew everything. What *did* I believe about prayer?

What he had said sounded reasonable. For several days,

every time I started to pray about something, I'd think, *Why bother? Everything is already planned.*

But I didn't feel happy. I didn't feel close to the Lord. And I didn't want to read the Bible. Something had broken my fellowship with Him.

After moping around for a week I decided that even though it was *possible* that prayer didn't change things, I'd still feel better if I talked it all over with Him. So I prayed:

"Dear Lord Jesus, I think You want me to pray—yet, You know how everything is going to end. Every hair on my head is numbered. And You know every time a sparrow falls. So why *should* I pray? Show me in Your Word, and increase my faith."

With the help of a concordance and the Bible the Lord answered my prayer. He showed me—

> *that we are to be like Jesus*—and how He prayed! (See John 17.)
> *that we are commanded to pray:* Jesus said we should always pray and not give up (Luke 18:1).
> *that it's a sin not to pray:* "Far be it from me that I should sin against the LORD by failing to pray for you (1 Sam. 12:23).
> *that prayer can change things:* "Peter therefore was kept in prison; but prayer was made without ceasing" (Acts 12:5 KJV). And he was released! (See vv. 7–11.)
> *that we should pray for salvation:* "God, have mercy on me, a sinner" (Luke 18:13).
> *that we should pray to confess sins:* "If we confess our sins, he is faithful and just and will forgive us our sins and purify us from all unrighteousness" (1 John 1:9).
> *that we should pray for wisdom:* "If any of you lacks wisdom, he should ask God, . . . and it will be given to him" (James 1:5).

that we should pray when we are sad: "I cry aloud to the LORD . . . I pour out my complaint before him" (Ps. 142:1–2).

that we should pray for power and victory over Satan: "I pray that you, . . . may have power" (Eph. 3:17–18). "Keep on praying for all saints" (Eph. 6:18).

that we should pray about EVERYTHING: "In everything, by prayer and petition, with thanksgiving, present your requests to God" (Phil. 4:6).

that prayer pleases God: "[prayer] is good, and pleases God our Savior" (2 Tim. 2:3).

And so I started to learn the purpose and meaning of prayer. We *should pray about* everything. And we can ask in *confidence!* This confidence that God hears and answers prayer is what I would most like to leave with you, my readers. As the writer of Hebrews tells us, "Let us then approach the throne of grace with confidence, so that we may receive mercy and find grace to help us in our time of need" (4:16).

This book records a sampling of hundreds of prayers I have asked and had answered. May God's faithfulness to me help you in your daily Christian walk.

Losses and Gains

I sat in the elevated chair, running my tongue around the sides of my flannel-dry mouth. *Why* I wondered, *does the dentist look so serious?*

"Well . . ." he sighed heavily. "I'm sorry, but your teeth need to be extracted."

I stared at him. My mouth opened. "You . . . mean . . . all of them?" *False teeth? Me?* I began to cry. For a young, vain woman nothing could have been worse.

All the next week I cried over the prospect of being *toothless!* But I had no choice. The following Monday morning I returned to the dreadful chair.

Gently, he pulled back my lips and injected novocain. "It will be a few minutes before I can start," he said.

"Do you mind if I smoke?" The tremulous voice didn't sound like mine.

"Not at all," he said. "I used to smoke."

Used to smoke, I thought. *Amazing.* I had to ask, "How did you quit?"

His blue eyes brightened and he grinned. He said he had always been self-sufficient, self-willed, and self-satisfied, but something had been missing in his life.

My first thought was, *Religious fanatic!* But I couldn't help being interested in what he was saying.

"When you accept something," he continued, "you simply reach out and take it, don't you? After I took Christ I discovered I had power to let go of the trash that cluttered my life."

I wanted to look away, but I couldn't. I saw something like sunshine around his head. I dropped my cigarette in the ashtray.

He began to probe in my mouth. "Do you believe you are a sinner?" he asked.

What a question! What timing. I tried to swallow and couldn't. Me? A sinner? I thought of my sophisticated life, the drinking parties, the deceit. "Yes," I answered.

He spoke softly. "What do you plan to do about this?"

I shrugged hopelessly. What could I do? Even if I could reform, the past was crimson.

"Somebody had to pay for sins," he said. "They used to kill animals as a sacrifice, but then Jesus Christ was crucified to pay everybody's bill." (I knew that. Did he think I was a heathen?) "The thing I didn't realize," he continued, "was that I had to admit I couldn't pay, and accept His sacrifice, without trying to add anything." He came closer, and I opened my mouth. "Can you accept the fact that Jesus died for your sins?"

I didn't answer, but the question burned in my mind. That evening I looked up the Scripture references he gave me. I couldn't wait for my next appointment!

I don't know when it was, but sometime before the last extraction, I knelt beside my bed and whispered:

"Dear Jesus, I'm a sinner. I'm sorry. Please forgive me. Thank You for what You did, and, if it covers my sins, I want to accept it."

I became a new person. Joy throbbed inside me. I awoke every morning thinking of Him. I couldn't talk very well with new dentures, but I couldn't keep quiet, either. I had to tell everybody what the dentist had told me.

Yet to all who received [accepted] him, to those who believed in his name, he gave the right to become children of God (John 1:12).

Mosquito Mastered

After I accepted Christ as my Savior, I was as happy as a bride on her honeymoon. But there was a mosquito in the bedroom, and it was tormenting me: I still smoked. The dentist had told me I would receive power to quit, but although I prayed over and over, I couldn't give up cigarettes. In fact, it seemed I smoked more. Each time I lit one, I felt the sting of guilt and shame. I had a lot of Christian friends, and I was the only one in that group who smoked.

My dentist assured me, "Don't worry about it. Right now you need to study the Bible. In time, all these things will fall away. After all, you were saved by faith—not by works!"

Weeks passed and I continued to argue with the Holy Spirit. When He told me it grieved Him for all that smoke to be in "our" lungs, I would say, "Lord, You know I want to quit. If You would just take away the desire, then I could."

With Christian friends I would excuse myself by saying, "I know I shouldn't smoke, but I can't quit. Anyway, we're saved by faith, you know—not by works."

One day I couldn't concentrate on my Bible reading. The cigarette in my hand distracted me. I jabbed it in the ashtray. I was under conviction, and I knew I would never be completely happy until I stopped arguing with the Lord. But how? I had tried. Once I had given them up for two days, but afterward I smoked more than ever. I couldn't imagine being happy—even in heaven—if I couldn't smoke.

13

Suddenly, the problem was unmasked: I couldn't quit because *I loved to smoke.* I *protected* my habit. I was like a mother with a spoiled child, always making excuses. Now, somehow, I had to turn myself around. I looked at the half-pack of cigarettes on the coffee table. I fondled the expensive lighter I'd received on my birthday. I placed it on the cigarettes and pushed them both away. I got on my knees beside the couch and prayed.

"Dear Lord, I've been a hypocrite. I keep telling You I want to quit and blaming You for not giving me power. The truth is I don't want to quit. I confess this to You. Please, in Your Name, I ask You to make me *hate* this habit. Make me hate the taste, the smell, and the thought of cigarettes. Let me see this habit from Your point of view."

When I threw the cigarettes in the trash I felt sad, as though a friend had died. But I wasn't going to argue with the Lord anymore.

It wouldn't be honest to say I didn't have a battle. Satan and my carnal spirit used all their tricks to try to make me start smoking again. But God gave me power—to read Christian literature after meals instead of reaching for that cigarette, to resist buying them, to say no when I was offered one. In a few weeks I actually *hated* the smell of cigarette smoke. And He has given me power to endure—for over twenty years! Praise Him.

[*Jesus said*] *"Why do you call me, 'Lord, Lord,' and do not do what I say?" (Luke 6:46).*

Yours for the Asking

After I became a Christian and began to talk about it, salvation almost became an epidemic in our family. All of our lives changed to some degree, but God had some radical alterations for two members of the family.

My nephew was just getting established in an accounting firm, with the goal of becoming a certified public accountant, when he accepted Christ. Suddenly his priorities changed; he began to study for the ministry.

Although we were amazed and thrilled at his decision, it wasn't long before he and his wife began to feel pinched financially. One day she confided, "Sometimes I get sick of being poor! I know I'm not poor in spiritual things, and I'm ashamed to complain—but look at this living room!"

It *was* a tiny room, in a tiny duplex. And the wooden couch, with faded cushions, had been designed for a patio. The rickety bookshelves, which covered most of one wall and held her husband's theology books, were nothing but old boards and bricks. An ugly, old-fashioned oak desk dominated the room. A plain rocker, without even a cushion, was the only other piece of furniture.

"I'll be so glad when he's out of seminary," she said, "Then maybe we can get some decent furniture."

The room *was* pitiful, and she looked pitiful, being big with child, yet pale and thin. I wanted so badly to help her, but we were almost as poor. Where could I go for help—except to the Lord?

"Let's pray right now for some furniture!" I said—with

false enthusiasm. "After all, this world is full of furniture! God knows where it is."

That was true, and I began to believe what I'd just said. He *could* supply it. As hope grew in me, belief sparkled in her eyes. We got on our knees and I spoke:

"Lord Jesus, we don't mean to be ungrateful. We are thankful for all you have already given to us, especially our salvation—but if there is any extra furniture around, we would appreciate it so much."

We rose from the floor, anticipating "furniture from heaven."

That very weekend a woman announced in Sunday school that she was redecorating and had bought new furniture. "Do you know anyone who needs a perfectly good living room set?"

Did I ever!

And what a difference that rose-colored velour couch and chair made in my niece's living room. God heard our prayer!

"Have faith in God," Jesus answered. "I tell you the truth, if anyone says to this mountain, 'Go, throw yourself into the sea,' and does not doubt in his heart but believes that what he says will happen, it will be done for him. Therefore I tell you, whatever you ask for in prayer, believe that you have received it, and it will be yours" (Mark 11:22–24).

Never Too Late

"After all," my mother said indignantly, "wasn't I the one who always took you and Dena to Sunday school and church?"

Her brown eyes flashed, and I remembered: that look meant "hush." But I couldn't keep quiet.

"Yes, but mother—"

"And *I* wasn't the one who smoked and drank!" She looked at me accusingly and her pretty mouth was an angry line.

"I know, mother, but—"

"I've always been a good woman! I'm not a sinner. I've gone to church all my life." See turned her fork around and around with her fingers. "When your daddy died I told everyone I didn't know how people who didn't have faith survived such times of need."

"But mother, are you really born again?"

It seemed every time my mother and I got together, we began to argue about salvation. I read Bible verses to her, and she could see my life had changed. And she could see the difference in my sister Dena, my son, Ron, and daughter, Joan, who had also been born again. She even said she believed the Bible, but when I asked her when *she* had accepted Christ, she always became angry.

This time she was so upset she jumped up from the table and stormed home.

After she slammed the front door I felt terrible. I went to the couch and got on my knees. With my eyes closed I pictured my sweet mother, condemned in eternal darkness; a good woman, but lost.

"Lord!" I cried. "You know mother is sixty-four. They say old people seldom change! Oh God, I beg of You, please save her before it's too late!"

I cried until there was a wet spot on the couch and my nose was red and swollen. Without feeling much relief, I went to the kitchen to do the lunch dishes. Just as I was putting away the last dish the phone rang. It was mother.

"Honey, I have to tell you something wonderful! All the way home I was so mad at you. It just made me furious to think you and Dena, after both of you had been so worldly, were now trying to be 'holier than thou.' But in my heart—"

She stopped and I knew she was fighting to keep from crying.

"—in my heart I knew you both had something I didn't. So as soon as I got home I went to the bedroom and said, 'Lord, I want whatever those girls have—no matter what it takes!' And honey, I think—" and her voice quavered, "you know what you've been pestering me about? I think I'm born again!"

Fantastic! While I had been crying for her to be saved, at that very moment, she had received a new life.

Surely the arm of the LORD is not too short to save, nor his ear too dull to hear (Isa. 59:1).

Passing the Plate

The pastor had preached a compelling message on tithes, offerings, and love gifts.

How I wished my husband had heard the sermon. He also had accepted Christ, but at that time he didn't seem as excited about "the way" as the rest of us. He skipped church often. But I usually tried to give him a rehash of the service.

"I'd like to give, honey," he said, "but let me show you some figures." He took a scratch pad and scribbled down our budget. It took all his salary to make the car and house payments, pay the utility bills and buy groceries. There wasn't even any money allotted for clothes. "You can see there isn't any to give."

Every week I felt sad an embarrassed when I let the offering plate pass me by. I was sure the ushers noticed, and little children, always intrigued by the offering, looked at me accusingly. I *had* to put in money! I began to take some of the grocery money, and, as a result, our plates had less meat and more noodles. Sometimes, by cutting out desserts and fruit, I managed to sneak out five or ten dollars. When my husband complained about the quality of our meals, I snapped back something about food prices.

One day he came home early and brought in the mail. One of the envelopes he opened was from church. It was a statement, showing we had contributed quite a bit that quarter.

"Why did you do it?" he demanded. "I told you we didn't have it! No wonder the meals have been so lousy!" His eyes were black with anger as he stormed outside.

What a mess I'd made of things, and I was only trying to please the Lord.

Wasn't I? Or was it *pride* that made me want to give?

I thought of the Scripture about wives being submissive to their husbands. I had not submitted. Besides that, I had been evasive, which was the same as lying. And I had cheated my family out of good meals. I felt so defeated and sinful, I began to cry.

"What can I do, Lord, to make it right? I really want to give to *You*, but there's no money, and now I've lost my husband's trust. Give me the strength to apologize, and please—make a way for us to bring our gifts to You."

Just as I was about to go outside and tell my husband I was sorry, he came in and led me to the table, where we both sat down.

"While I was out in the garage, I was thinking," he said. "I know we should be giving to the church, so, although I don't know what will happen, you can give twenty-five dollars a month. That's not much, but it's a start."

I jumped up and hugged him.

"But no more," he admonished, "until I get out of debt."

That night, before I went to sleep, I thanked the Lord over and over. Twenty-five dollars wasn't a tenth of what my husband earned, but it was what he was willing to give. I was determined to be submissive (with the Lord's help!) from then on.

At last, I could relax about the amount I could give to the Lord.

For if the willingness is there, the gift is acceptable according to what one has, not according to what he does not have (2 Cor. 8:12).

Giving Gifts

"How shall we celebrate Christmas this year? I asked Dena.

"You mean now that we're Christians?" she said.

"Yes," I said. "This is the first Christmas we've really known the Christ of Christmas. I know one thing—I'm not going to have another rowdy party on Christmas Eve."

"Oh no," she agreed. "I think we should still have fun, but everything should honor the Lord."

"In our decorating too." I said. "I think I'll buy a nativity set for the coffee table instead of that ceramic Santa Claus."

"Good idea," Dena replied. "I plan to send Christmas cards with Bible verses on them."

"And how about a cake that says 'Happy Birthday, Jesus'?" I said.

We got excited as we planned ways to celebrate and decorate that would point our friends and neighbors toward the Lord. As Christmas drew near, it seemed I thought of Him all the time. He had given up His home in glory to come to this polluted planet. He lived among people who didn't give a snap of their fingers for Him. He voluntarily died an excruciating death, to pay for their—for my—sins. He gave His life. I wanted to give also. But how? There was never an extra nickel.

One television station kept showing a telephone number to call if you wanted to help a poor family have a better Christmas.

"But I keep telling you," my husband said, "*we're* a poor family! We'll have to buy the kids' presents on credit as it is."

I took the problem to the Lord:

"Lord Jesus, You know my heart. I would like to help a family this year—but I'm not going to try anything deceitful, like taking money from the food budget. Help us find a way not only to give food for their bodies, but also the gospel. I'm ready, if You'll provide the way."

Seeing that telephone number on the TV screen so often was as painful to me as being stuck by a sharp needle, but there was nothing I could do. I had our food planned down to the last box of Jell-O.

Then, about three days before Christmas, an avalanche of Christmas cards tumbled through the mailslot, onto the carpet. I looked quickly at the return addresses. I came to a small, soiled envelope addressed to us in pencil. It was from my husband's eighty-two-year-old father. I opened it. There wasn't a note inside, but four twenty-dollar bills fell out. Bless his heart! And all I'd sent him was a box of cookies and fudge.

With my husband's permission, I called that telephone number. They gave me the name of a needy widow with two small children; that evening we took twenty dollars worth of groceries and a few toys to that sad little family. The Lord had made a way for us to give! Oh, yes—in one of the bags of groceries I slipped a tract entitled: "The True Meaning of Christmas."

Thanks be to God for His indescribable gift! (2 Cor. 9:15).

Heartache

One foggy morning I watched my husband back his car down the driveway, turn the corner, and disappear. My heart actually began to ache. This business trip would take him a thousand miles away from me. My mind stumbled ahead, through the weeks of being both mother and father, the full responsibility of the home, and the loneliness of an empty bed.

There wasn't even a specific homecoming date to anticipate; "When the job is done," he had said. How could I face it? I clenched my fists hard and dug my fingernails into my palms. Hot tears, held back until he was out of sight, flowed down my cheeks.

"Oh Lord," I murmured as I stood on the front porch and stared into the fog, "I can't stand this! I can't bear this loneliness! Take it away, please. I can't face it unless You take this pain away."

After the children had gone to school the phone rang. It was the Women's Missionary Council president.

"Didn't you tell me your husband was going out of town?" she said.

"Yes." I said. "In fact, he just left this morning." I could feel tears starting up again.

"I was wondering," she went on, "since you'll probably have some extra time, if you'd be willing to make the table decorations for our yearly mother and daughter banquet?"

Handcraft, in fact, any kind of art, is a joy to me. I eagerly said, "Yes!"

23

"I'll bring the supplies over and you can start whenever you want," she said.

The Lord had more plans to cushion the pain of loneliness. The pastor telephoned. "Could you team up with one of the women and go calling every Tuesday?" When I hesitated, he added, "You'll only be calling on women who have visited the church and indicated on the attendance card they'd like someone to stop by. It will be a blessing for you, and an opportunity for spiritual growth."

And the Lord had even more plans!

"Mother, since we're going to the banquet." Joan suggested, "why not make dresses alike?"

"Would you consider teaching third-grade girls for two Sundays?" one of my friends asked. "We're going on vacation, and I need somebody to take my place."

With all the extra activity the days snapped by so fast and I was so exhausted at night that I had no time to feel sad or lonely. I barely had time to write my husband. I was tempted to say, "Hold it, Lord!" But He was gracious and kind to keep me so busy. When my husband came home, it was hard to believe he'd been gone a month and two days!

I, even I, am he who comforts you (Isa. 51:12).

Old Flames

The telephone rang. "Is this Mab?"

"Yes," I said. "Who's this?"

"Dick Leatherton. Do you remember me?"

Did I remember! My mind zoomed back to eleventh grade. I'd been madly in love with him.

He filled me in on the past several years. He was married, with two children about the same ages as our teenagers, Ron and Joan. And he had recently been transferred to our city.

"My wife and I would love to have you and your family come for dinner," he said. "How about this Sunday?"

After church we drove to their house. I was impressed. This was no tract neighborhood, like ours. A picturesque and expensive brick walk curved through exotic tropicals and shrubbery to a big house.

Dick and his wife came to the door, smiling graciously. She looked glamorous in her expensive hostess gown. I felt frumpy in my homemade dress. And their children looked like pictures in a Sears catalogue!

"Come in, come in!" Dick boomed, as he ushered us into an entry hall almost as big as Joan's bedroom.

The furniture, carpets, pictures—everything was beautiful and expensive. Even their snooty dog had a pedigree. Dick had done well.

"About six months ago the company made me a division manager." He gave us his charming smile.

I groaned inwardly. He was so handsome! A little

heavier, but the same charisma. I could have had all this! We had been practically engaged for a while. I burned with envy.

After a gourmet dinner, we sat in their spacious living room, drank coffee from antique cups, and listened to his wife tell about her clubs, lodges, and various honors. I felt utterly miserable. And worried. Wouldn't I have to return their invitation? What would they think of our tiny "shack" and worn-out furniture?

"Well, Ron," Dick turned his brilliant blue eyes on our son. "Jeff, here, plans to be a doctor. What are you going to do with your life?"

"I'm not positive," Ron said, looking directly at Dick, "but I've been thinking about becoming a preacher." His face was bright, as though a spotlight were on him. I was proud of him. Suddenly, the light seemed to turn on me, and I saw myself as God did. Self-centered, self-conscious. Why, I hadn't even thought of telling them about Christ! Instead I had allowed Satan to take hold of me, sensually and materially, and he was squeezing the life out of me. He was choking me with jealousy. I needed to be rescued! I closed my eyes a moment and prayed silently:

"Oh, God! I'm so jealous! I'm coveting, but I can't seem to help it. Please, Lord! Take over in my life, right now!"

"Well, that's great!" Dick blustered. "Religion never hurt anyone. Of course, I work on most Sundays—and if I do have a free weekend, we like to take off for Vegas.

His lovely wife nodded, and at that moment I realized the Lord had broken Satan's strangle hold. I looked around at their showcase home, and my jealousy was gone. I was *content.* They had possessions, but we have the Lord.

Do not store up for yourselves treasures on earth. . . . Store up for yourselves treasures in heaven. . . . For where your treasure is, there your heart will be also (Matt. 6:19–21).

Following the Leader

"How about taking your turn leading the Bible study next month?" our Women's Missionary Council president asked one Sunday.

My mouth opened and I blinked. I had attended W.M.C. meetings, and I loved the fellowship and Bible study. I knew the women took turns doing the lessons, but somehow it had never occurred to me that I would be asked.

"Oh, no," I protested. "I couldn't. I don't know that much about the Bible."

"You don't have to," she said, smiling. She showed me a couple of mimeographed sheets. "See, the lesson is already mapped out. All you have to do is study it until the Holy Spirit speaks to you; then you speak to us!"

"I can't speak in public," I whined. "I almost fainted once when I tried to give a testimony."

"But this isn't the same! You know all of us. We're just like you." She stuck the sheets in my Bible. "I'm not going to take no for an answer." She hugged me and walked away.

I was encouraged by her faith in me, but the thought of standing up in front of people actually made me sick.

"Why do I have such stage fright?" I asked my mother.

"Probably because you're too concerned with what people think of you," she said. "Forget yourself and concentrate on the lesson."

It was good advice, but the more I prepared, the more my stomach convulsed.

I practiced in front of a mirror. I prayed about it several times a day, but I was so afraid, I couldn't concentrate on prayer.

The morning of the meeting I awoke with dread, as though someone had died. How could I get through the meeting? In four hours I'd be standing in front of the women. My heart began such a violent thudding I wondered if I were having a heart attack. In agony I cried out:

"Oh Lord! Forgive me for being so self-centered, but I can't help it! I know I'm going to make a big mess of this devotion unless you take over, right now!"

My heart quit pounding, and once more I was determined to practice what I was going to say. I read aloud the verse we were to memorize:

"But thanks be to God, who always leads us in triumphal procession in Christ and through us spreads everywhere the fragrance of the knowledge of him" (2 Cor. 2:14).

I knew the verse, but for the first time two words turned on like a neon sign: *always* and *leads.* The game "Follow the Leader" came to mind. God was *always* the *Leader.* He was going to walk ahead of me, down the steps of the front porch, into the car. He was going to precede me up the steps of the church and into the Fellowship Hall. He would stand in front of me at the lectern. My friends would see *Him,* not me! Fear gradually seeped away and was replaced by a tremulous anticipation. I had prepared. I knew what to say. But He would enable me to speak coherently.

And He did. Several women complimented me, but the praise went to the Lord.

Now when I give talks, I still have stage fright, but none of that awful dread. I know He always leads the way.

Dread not, neither be afraid.... The LORD your God who goeth before you, he shall fight for you (Deut. 1:29–30 KJV).

Good News!

"How would you like to go with me Saturday to a demonstration of how to teach children in your own home, using visual aids?" asked the pastor's sister, Edith.

The thought of teaching little children didn't seem too appealing, but I went anyway, to please Edith.

After chicken à la king and gelatin, a vibrant, plump, and pretty woman taught us a couple of children's songs about Jesus, then another woman crossed the platform to an easel. On it rested a large, soft-looking painting of a green river and bushes, with bright, blue sky over head. It was the first time I'd ever seen a flannelgraph background. The teacher had a paper-doll Pharaoh's daughter march down to the river and find the cut-out baby Moses behind the flannel bush. I was hooked! I wanted to tell flannelgraph stories too. I listened avidly and wrote down the time we could go to classes in our own neighborhood.

But there was a catch. Money. Or rather, the lack of it.

"All these materials can be purchased here," the woman said, "or in your Christian bookstore. If you're artistic, you can paint your own backgrounds." I could do that, I thought. I'd done quite a lot of oil painting.

"But don't use oils," she went on, "because the paint dries hard and the figures won't stick to it. You can't use crayons either, because they aren't bright enough. You really need these." She held up a box of special crayons. They're as bright as oils, but allow the flannel to stay soft and fluffy." Then she told the price of each necessary item.

The total was more than I spent for groceries in a week!

"How did you like it?" Edith asked on the way home.

"I love it," I answered, sadly. "I'd love to teach the kids on our block, but we simply don't have the money right now."

That night after dinner I took out water colors and art paper and made Pharaoh's daughter and baby Moses. Next I glued bits of flannel on the backsides, and then I told the story, using the back of the couch for my flannelboard. My husband and children were fascinated! Joanie was eager to play the piano for me, and Ron offered his help. But there was no money in our budget for equipment.

Before I went to sleep that night all those figures marched around in my mind: Baby Moses, his sister Miriam, and Pharaoh's daughter.

"Dear Lord, I really want to teach a Good News Club! I can make the figures myself, and the backgrounds too, but I have to have an easel. Surely, You've put this desire in my heart, so I know You'll provide the way."

The next week, for my birthday, Edith and two other friends took me to lunch. The subject of Good News Clubs came up, and I told them how much I wanted to teach.

"Right now, there's just no way. But I've asked the Lord, so I'm sure if He wants me to teach, He'll make the way."

All three of them laughed, and Edith reached down beside her and pulled up a huge package. They had pooled their money and bought an easel, flannelboard, the special crayons, and two lessons!

"Jehovah-jireh!" Edith said.

"What does that mean? I asked, when I could speak.

"The Lord will provide!"

Day after day, in the temple courts and from house to house, they never stopped teaching and proclaiming the good news that Jesus is the Christ (Acts 5:42).

Both Feet on the Ground

"The company wants me to visit their plant in Denver," my husband said one evening. "Want to go with me?"

"How exciting!" I said. "Would we drive?"

"Oh no, we'd fly," he replied.

Fly! I was terrified of flying. I was the only adult in our family who'd never been up in an airplane. I didn't want to go if we had to fly, but what could I say? Hadn't I told everyone I knew that since I was a Christian all fears were gone? Where was my faith? I put on a sickly smile.

"I'm glad you want to go," he said. "I have to be there for a week, and I'd be lonely without you."

The next few days were a nightmare. Over and over I imagined myself walking into the airplane. All the doors and windows would be locked. Then I would be strapped in a seat. Suddenly we would zoom up, up, thousands of feet in the air. There would be nothing underneath us. The thought always caused me to break out in a cold sweat and a lump to form in my stomach. I looked up Bible verses on fear, but it didn't help. I couldn't even pray!

I went to see our pastor. I told him about the business trip and the fact I had never been in an airplane. "I'm ashamed, but I'm just sick with fear!"

He smiled kindly and pointed to a plaque on his study wall. "Thou wilt keep him in perfect peace, whose mind is stayed on thee: because he trusteth in thee" (Isa. 26:3 KJV).

I read it aloud and then shook my head. "I can't seem to get it," I said.

He read the verse, enunciating each word distinctly. Then he said, "Do you know what 'stayed' means? It means to have your thoughts glued on Christ. Don't think about the flight or your fear of flying. Think about Him. Does He have power to take care of you only on the ground? Or is He also able to take care of you in the air, which, by the way, He created?"

I smiled. Although my fears weren't completely gone, I could see how unreasonable they were. He wrote some Bible references on a piece of scratch paper.

"Read these verses when you get home. Try to memorize them. When anxiety comes, put it down—with the Word." When he handed me the piece of paper, he reminded me of a doctor giving a prescription.

At home I typed every verse on index cards. I read them over and over; I began to see how insulting I had been to the Lord. My fear was like saying, "I don't trust You, Lord!" Ashamed, I prayed:

"Heavenly Father! God of the universe, forgive me for being afraid. Forgive me for not trusting You to keep me, as though You are not capable, whether I am in the air or on the ground. From this moment I trust You. Fill me with Your perfect peace."

Waiting in line to board, a moment of panic seized me. *What am I doing here,* I thought as I looked out the window at the huge plane. For a second I considered running away, then I remembered my prayer. Did I trust Him? I had *asked* for His peace. All fear left.

My first flight was wonderful, and I even enjoyed the meal!

There is no one like the God of Jeshurun, who rides on the heavens to help you, and on the clouds in his majesty. The eternal God is your refuge, and underneath are the everlasting arms (Deut. 33:26–27).

Okay? Okay. Okay!

One Sunday the superintendent of the primary department in our Sunday school trotted over to my car just as I was about to leave the church grounds. "Have you ever thought about teaching Sunday school?" she panted.

"No!" I barked. "Please! A Good News Club is enough kids for me!"

Her eyes met mine and she nodded sympathetically. She sighed then, and said, "Would you pray about this? I have to get somebody to teach third-grade girls." She smiled wistfully. "I was sure you'd say yes!"

"You know I work as secretary in the church office now." My voice sounded accusing.

"I know. And I know it would be hard on you. But there are several of us who have full-time jobs, and yet the Lord seems to make enough time." She squeezed my arm. "All I ask is that you pray about it, okay?"

"Okay," I promised. On the way home I grumbled to the Lord. "How can I teach, Lord? Keeping house for four is a full-time job, and I work every day at the church, and I teach the Good News Club once a week." I'd heard of Christians who got so involved in church work they got disgusted and quit doing anything. I didn't want that to happen to me. And another thing: my husband was not as interested in the church as I. He might become rebellious.

The next morning, however, before I went to work, I prayed:

"Lord Jesus, I want to do what You want me to, yet I'm

sure You already have me doing all I'm supposed to. Surely, You don't want me to get too busy, do you? In Jesus' name, Amen."

I got ready to leave the house, but something was wrong. I tried to sing, but couldn't think of the first line of any chorus. I went back to the bedroom and prayed again:

"Lord, this time I submit to You. If You want me to teach that third-grade girls' class—well, okay! But just make Your will clear."

After the prayer, I felt good. I don't think anything makes you as happy as knowing everything is all right between you and the Lord.

That Saturday, my sister Dena and I were sitting down to lunch, when Joan and a little neighbor girl came in.

"Carla's mom wants me to keep an eye on her for a couple hours," Joan explained.

"Well, there's plenty to eat," I said. "Come on Carla, sit by me."

Most of the conversation during the meal was about the Lord, the Bible, and church. During a lull, Carla said softly, "Everybody at this table is a Christian but me."

If a magic genie had risen out of the Fritos, we couldn't have been more surprised. Right here at our table was a little person asking to be saved! Of course we led her to Christ. Of course she was a third grade girl. And, of course, I realized this was God's answer to my prayer.

When Joan and Carla left the room, I said to Dena, "Guess what? I'm going to be teaching a Sunday school class."

It was he who gave some to be apostles, some to be prophets, some to be evangelists, and some to be pastors and teachers, to prepare God's people for works of service, so that the body of Christ may be built up (Eph. 4:11–12).

34

Opposing Forces

One Wednesday evening during dinner, the doorbell rang. Joan answered the door, then called: "There's a man here, mother. He wants to talk to you."

He was a stranger—about thirty-five, lean, and good-looking. Judging from his plaster-dusted blue jeans and dirty sweat shirt, he was a laborer.

"You the lady teaches them religious stories?"

I'd been holding weekly Good News Club meetings in my living room. Up to thirty neighborhood children crowded in to hear Bible stories and sing songs. *He must be one of the parents,* I thought.

"Yes! Come on in." I started to open the screen door. Maybe he was going to compliment me!

"No thanks," he said curtly. "I'm Greg McIntyre's dad."

"Greg! Oh! Greg is my star pupil!"

Mr. McIntyre didn't smile. "I don't want him comin' here no more. We have our own religion, and we don't want our kids taught no strange cult."

"But Mr. McIntyre, the gospel isn't—"

He shook his finger, and his eyes narrowed to angry slits. "Just see to it! He's not to come here no more!" His face looked ugly as he turned to walk away. I felt insulted, angry, and frustrated—even persecuted.

When I returned to the table, my husband looked stern. He got up and poured himself coffee. "Maybe you ought to quit teaching the neighbor kids. Just seems to cause problems," he said.

35

"Are you telling me to quit?" I blurted out. I was immediately sorry. "If you tell me I have to, of course I will."

"I'm not telling you to. Your conscience has to be your guide. I just hate to have the neighbors down on us."

The next morning I asked Him what I should do:

"Dear Lord Jesus, You know I don't want to stop having a Good News Club. I love the kids. But, I don't want to be a troublemaker either. Oh, Father! What shall I do?"

In an instant Matthew 19:14 flashed in my head: "Jesus said, 'Let the little children come to me, and do not hinder them, for the kingdom of heaven belongs to such as these.'"

That was my answer! Of course, I would continue the Good News Club. As for Greg, I would have to comply with his father's wishes.

The next Wednesday Greg came to the door for the class. "Greg—I can't let you in. Your daddy doesn't want you to be here."

I almost cried when I saw two fat tears form in his eyes. All during class he sat outside the screen door and listened. It almost broke my heart. After class I gave him a cookie and said, "Greg, you already have Jesus in your heart. Now you must be a good soldier for Him. So even though you'd like to be with us, it's a braver thing for you to obey your dad. Okay?"

He looked up at me and his little shoulders lifted, then sagged. "Okay." His feet dragged as he headed home.

Greg never came back, but I know I'll see him, along with my other little friends, in heaven.

Blessed are you when people insult you, persecute you and falsely say all kinds of evil against you because of me. Rejoice and be glad, because great is your reward in heaven, for in the same way they persecuted the prophets who were before you (Matt. 5:11–12).

My Jerusalem

Our pastor's Bible was in his left hand. He read from it distinctly: "But you will receive power when the Holy Spirit comes on you; and you will be my witnesses in Jerusalem, and in all Judea and Samaria, and to the ends of the earth (Acts 1:8).

He looked at the congregation. His dark eyes seemed to peer into my mind. We were in for it, I was sure.

"The Lord told His disciples to go first to the people in their own town of Jerusalem." He closed his Bible and walked around to the front of the pulpit.

"Some of you have told me you're willing to go to the mission field—but you haven't witnessed to your neighbors."

I relaxed. The people on each side of us and across the street had heard the gospel.

"Let's not talk of foreign fields," the pastor said, "until we've told the people on our own block."

Our own block meant at least fifty families for me! Did he mean every house?

"Your block is your Jerusalem."

At work the next day I said, "Pastor, I'm going to put a salvation tract in every mailbox on our block." I waited for his approval.

"Better not," he warned. "It's against the law."

"Hmm. In that case, I guess I can't do it," I said.

"You could knock on each door," he replied. "Smile at them, give them a tract, and invite them to church."

He grinned and I groaned. "I couldn't do that!" I said.

37

He shrugged. He never pushed anyone into service. He let the Holy Spirit do the talking.

I tried to forget the idea, but before I went home, I went to the tract rack and carefully made a selection. Then I stepped into the sanctuary and sat down in a back pew.

"Lord Jesus," I whispered. "I dread the thought of distributing these tracts. It seems so fanatical, but, if this is what You want, please give me courage. Also, please protect me. Just make the way smooth, Lord, and let them accept the Word gladly."

When I got home I combed my hair, repaired my make-up, and started out. No one was home at the first two houses, and I tucked the leaflets inside the screen doors, but at the third house the woman insisted I come in and explain my belief to her!

When I left her house I felt giddy.

Nothing exciting happened the rest of that afternoon. Either the people weren't home, or they politely accepted the literature.

It actually took three afternoons to cover my block. But I felt wonderful—so alive and joyful! I talked to many women. I eagerly told an alcoholic, who, for three years, had hidden inside her home to keep from disgracing her family, how the Lord had saved and delivered me. A woman in a wheelchair, the mother of a lovable mongoloid boy, accepted my offer to take him to church, where he received Christ. Another mother let me pick up her daughter every Sunday.

How wonderfully and specifically the Lord answered my prayer. He gave me the courage to go through with it and He protected me from any unpleasantness.

My Jerusalem was now in God's hands.

As it is written, "How beautiful are the feet of those who bring good news!" (Rom. 10:15).

To Whom Am I Speaking?

One day several of us women were having lunch in the church kitchen and sharing our testimonies and experiences. I told about the time a friend, Leah, had demonstrated Christ's presence by patting the couch cushion between us and declaring He was there. "He was so real to me," I said. "From then on I believed He not only was my Savior, Friend, and Father, but like my husband, too."

Most of the women smiled and nodded, but one frowned. "It's good to have an intimate relationship with the Lord," she said, "but it's also important to remember *who* He is. Although He is our Savior, He is still God of very God."

"Here in America," she continued, "we are so democratic that it's hard to think of Him as Almighty God. But the Bible calls us servants of the King. It's only His goodness that has allowed us to be free; actually, our relationship to God is that of a slave."

I felt chastised. Had I been too familiar with the Lord? I asked the Lord's forgiveness. He was the Great God of the universe and I had treated Him as a member of the family—popping in and out with all kinds of ridiculous requests; complaining about the weather, the kids, the work. As my Savior, Friend, Father, and Husband, I had shared with Him every thought that flitted through my brain. As His servant, His slave, I had no right to assume so much. From now on, I promised, I would regard Him as sovereign King.

My prayer life changed. I felt stiff and formal with Him, and I lost the joy of our close relationship. Daily devotions became a chore, and some of my old fears crept back. I knew God loved me; I knew I was saved, but, after all, if I was a slave He *might* cut me off. From salvation? No, I didn't think so, yet—. What had happened to my assurance?

One night, several weeks after that kitchen luncheon, I began to pray in the old, familiar way:

"Hello, Lord. I don't know what's happened to me. I can't seem to get close to You anymore. Is it because I don't like the idea of being a servant? I don't know. It isn't that I don't want to serve you. I just miss 'climbing up in Your lap' and calling You 'Father.' I used to be sure You enjoyed my company, too. Now I wonder if I insulted You all those times when I talked to You about everything—no matter how personal. Dear God, is this how You want it? Won't you please look down from Your throne and tell me what my relationship with You is?"

The next morning a part of John 5:39 came to mind: "Study the Scriptures" It was an answer from the King! After concentrated study I was again filled with the *joy* of the Lord. Jesus had said:

1. He is my Friend: "I no longer call you servants, because a servant does not know his master's business. Instead, I have called you *friends*" (John 15:15).

2. He is my Father: "Anyone who has seen me has seen the *Father*" (John 14:9).

3. He is my Husband: Jesus told the disciples He was going to prepare a place for us. And John, in Revelation 21:9, calls that place "the bride, the *wife* of the Lamb."

What a fantastic thought: He *is* King, and I'm a queen!

Yet, O LORD, you are our Father. . . . we are all the work of your hand (Isa. 64:8).

The Eyes Have It

Our daughter Joan wore contact lenses in high school, and although I loved how she looked in them, sometimes I thought a curse must have come with the guarantee; she was forever losing one. As soon as she would scream "I've lost a lens!" we would all freeze, while she crept around on her hands and knees feeling the floor. More often than not, after we'd given up hope, she would find it where it belonged—in her eye.

One day she was at the beach with the church group and, while they were sitting around talking, it happened.

"My contact! It's gone!" she cried. "It flew right out of my eye!"

"Are you sure?" a friend asked. "Maybe it's still in your eye."

"No, no," she moaned. "It's gone! The wind flipped it away."

Gary, one of the fellows in the group, shouted "Don't anyone move! "The Lord knows where it is. We'll ask Him to show us."

In the silence that followed, oblivious to the sunbathers around him, he prayed:

"Lord Jesus, You know everything. You know where Joan's lens is. Lord, please show it to us."

Joan said when she opened her eyes and felt the sea breeze, all her hope and faith vanished. She appreciated Gary's prayer, but that tiny lens *had* to have blown far away.

Gary turned slightly, and his eyes focused on something just to the right of Joan's towel. He gasped, "There it is!"

He reached out carefully as though it might fly away like a frightened bird, and from a million grains of sand he picked up a transparent disc smaller than a dime—and it wasn't even scratched.

Are not five sparrows sold for two pennies? Yet not one of them is forgotten by God. Indeed, the very hairs of your head are all numbered.... You are worth more than many sparrows (Luke 12:6–7).

Match Breaker?

When our daughter Joan was a sophomore in high school she fell in love with a senior. He was a football hero, and, according to her, the most handsome man in the world.

"Is he a Christian?" I asked.

"Mother! You talk like I'm going to marry him!"

I raised my eyebrows. "It could happen. A lot of people meet in high school and eventually marry."

One afternoon she burst into the house with a shout: "Phil asked me to go to the show some night!"

She was so ecstatic I hated to spoil it, but I had to ask, "Did you find out what he believes?"

"No!" she shouted. She had always been an obedient child, and I was shocked at her tone. "Wow, Mother! You can't start right in giving him the third degree!"

I felt apprehensive. One of the women at church had a son who'd become so rebellious he had run away. I didn't want to drive Joan from me, but I had to guide her. How could I without making her angry?

"Joanie, invite him here for lunch Saturday. You know we can't let you date him until we meet him."

Saturday we fixed a gourmet lunch, including Joan's cream puffs. When Phil came to the door I saw why she had fallen so hard.

At the lunch table, somewhere between salad and cream puffs, I asked, "Where do you go to church, Phil?"

"I don't," he said as he flashed his charming smile. "I

had all the religion I could take when I was a kid. I don't need it now."

I started to retort, but Joan gave me such a pleading look, I kept quiet. Maybe I *was* overly protective. After lunch I excused them and did the dishes by myself.

While I was wiping off the stove, Joan came out to the kitchen and whispered, "He wants me to go to the show tomorrow night!"

"Sunday night?" I whispered. Then I prayed:

"Oh God! Guide me. She's in love with him. I don't want to drive her away, but he's not right for her. Tell me what to do!"

In a flash He gave me a wise answer. Calmly, I said, "Joan, invite him to come to church with you tomorrow.

"Mother!" she protested. I motioned her to be quiet.

"If he comes to church, you may go with him tomorrow night."

Her eyes widened, then she flounced out of the kitchen.

In about fifteen minutes his car roared away. Joan went to her room and slammed the door. My heart ached. Had I done the wrong thing? I sat down in the living room and hoped the Spirit was praying—I couldn't.

About an hour later Joan came and sat beside me. "You know what he did when I invited him to church?" she asked. Her eyes and nose were red. "He *laughed.*"

We sat in silence for a while. I reached over and took her hand. She squeezed mine. After a few moments she spoke. "I was mad at you, Mother. But you were right. After he laughed at our church, I knew he wasn't for me."

(There is a happy ending. Joan met Don, a fine Christian man, in Bible College. They married, and are serving Jesus together.)

For the LORD gives wisdom, and from his mouth come knowledge and understanding (Prov. 2:6).

44

Deep and Wide

Our marriage was in trouble. For several years there'd been signs that we were not the loving couple we'd once been. I see now in retrospect, I was too absorbed in church and our teenagers' schedules to give much thought to the distance growing between us. Naturally, when I did give it any thought, I put the blame on him. Although he had apparently accepted Christ about the same time I did, little by little, he had quit reading the Bible, started avoiding church, and became critical of our Christian friends.

We quarreled a lot, and, when he began to smoke and drink again, my heart almost broke. I had to tell someone, so I talked to my friend, Leah.

"Let's pray hard for him and show more love," she said.

"I'm not sure I do love him anymore," I confessed. "And, when he's been drinking, I'm scared of him."

"There was a time, awhile back, when I thought I didn't love Jay," Leah said shyly. "In fact, I could hardly stand him!" She laughed out loud. "It wasn't that he was doing anything wrong—I just wanted to love the Lord and not be bothered with Jay. Isn't that awful? He showed me that I was supposed to be my husband's helpmate, so I asked the Lord to give me an extra portion of His love for Jay."

"Did he?" I asked.

She nodded emphatically. "Even now, if I start feeling irritated with him, I pray again for more love. We're supposed to be submissive and show love to our husbands; were not to sit and judge them."

I didn't answer. I felt cross.

"Maybe you're going to church too much. He might be jealous, with you working there, being in the choir, teaching—"

After she went home, I kept thinking about asking for love. Maybe it would work. I couldn't honestly say I was submissive to him in all areas. I hadn't really loved him either, since he began to smoke again. Sadly, I thought things might have been different if I had spent more time with him instead of always flouncing out the door with an attitude that almost shouted, *I'm better than you because I'm going to church.* What a Pharisee I had become. With tears in my eyes I prayed:

"Lord Jesus, I've sinned. I've pretended to be submissive when I haven't been. I've manipulated things to get my way, and I've been stormy and ugly and unloving. Please forgive me. And now I ask you for a deep, wide portion of *Your* love for my husband."

That night when I heard him come in the door, I rushed to meet him. I gave him a big kiss—on the mouth. I smelled liquor, but it didn't make me angry. I only felt sorry that he had to have something to cheer him up before coming home. Unfortunately, he'd already had so much cheer he didn't feel like eating the expensive beef roast I had prepared. He hurried to the bathroom, where wave after wave of nausea hit him. Compassion and love, absolutely from the Lord, flowed through me, and I brought him a chair. When the awful sickness was over, I bathed his face, helped undress him, and put him to bed. As I covered him, I realized this was God's love in action. The Lord had given me an overflowing portion of His agape love.

Love is patient, love is kind.... It is not easily angered, it keeps no record of wrongs (1 Cor. 13:4–5).

Oh Yes! Maybe!

One evening my husband asked if I would mind his inviting to dinner two Japanese men who were visiting his company.

"Oh, invite them," I urged. "I just hope I can serve something they'll eat." I knew nothing about Japanese cuisine, but I would try.

"Oh—one more thing. They don't speak English. One of them can say a few words, but the other one—nothing!"

The pastor's wife was a terrific cook, so I talked to her.

"Honey, I wouldn't worry about the meal. Just thank the Lord for bringing a mission field right into your home."

I hadn't thought of that! Maybe we could figure out a way to tell them about Jesus—that is, if my husband would agree. I went to prayer.

"Dear Lord, I'm praying about three things. First, that you would soften my husband's heart, so he'll agree to let us talk about Christ; second, that You would show us *how*. And third, oh Lord! Tell me what to fix for dinner."

That night I asked my husband if it would be all right to tell the men about Jesus.

"Of course, I think it would be appropriate, because this is a Christian nation."

(Number one answered!)

"I really don't know how to go about it though," I said, "since they don't speak English."

"Isn't there some kind of Japanese literature?"

"Oh Yes! The American Bible Society!"

(Number two answered.)

When I told my neighbor about our guests I said, "The only thing is, I don't know what to serve."

"Why not a typical American meal? If you were in Japan wouldn't you want to sample their food? How about turkey, with all the trimmings?"

(Number three answered! I knew how to cook turkey.)

It was obvious our guests enjoyed the food, because they took seconds of everything. The one who could speak a few words tried to interpret for the other one. No matter what we said, they both nodded and smiled, and the spokesman always answered, "Oh yes! Maybe!"

"I hope you like turkey?" I said when we first sat down.

"Oh yes! Maybe!"

"Do you think I could learn Japanese?"

"Oh yes! Maybe!"

After dinner I wondered how I would give them the Japanese New Testaments. They made the opportunity. The spokesman took a tiny box out of his pocket, came to stand before me, bowed low, and gave it to me. Inside was a pair of pearl earrings. I squealed with delight and put them on immediately. Now it was my turn. I said a quick prayer for the Japanese tracts tucked inside, and handed them the gifts. With obvious surprise, they untied the ribbons. They were probably Buddhists, and I hoped it wouldn't anger them. But they seemed delighted. They spoke to each other rapidly, nodding their heads. Then they bowed to us.

"Thank you," the spokesman said. "We like much."

The other one nodded and smiled, almost to his ears. "Oh yes! Maybe."

Do not forget to entertain strangers, for by so doing some people have entertained angels without knowing it (Heb. 13:2).

Things Not Seen

I usually spent a few minutes each day talking to the man who delivered the mail to the church office, where I worked as secretary. One day I said, "Jake, how about coming to church Sunday? You like the preacher, so I know you'd enjoy hearing him speak."

He took off his billed cap and without looking at me he answered, "I'm Jewish, you know."

"I know—but Jesus was Jewish."

"We don't believe in Jesus. And we believe in one God."

"We believe in only one God, Jake. Wish you'd come hear the pastor explain it."

We bantered back and forth, day after day. Jake took my witnessing good naturedly, but I got nowhere.

One day when I saw him coming toward the church, I knelt beside my desk and quickly prayed:

"Father, Jake is one of your *chosen ones*. Help me not waste words today, but give me courage to tell him plainly that he is a sinner and needs Jesus to save him."

I jumped up and grabbed the Bible. My hands trembled as I tried to remember exactly where the passage was that told about Paul's conversion. By the time Jake plopped his heavy mail sack on my desk, I was ready for him. "Jake, can you take time to listen to something?"

"Sure," he said and immediately sat down.

"I'm going to read an account of another Jewish man. He believed in the one God so much he went around persecuting Christians."

49

"Oh, oh," Jake said and looked up at me from under his dark eyebrows. I smiled and then read from Acts 9.

He listened attentively. When I was finished, we were both silent. At last he said, "Geez! I'd hate to be blind for three days."

"Does Paul's experience make you believe in Christ?"

He picked up the mail sack.

"I told you. Jews don't believe that New Testament story. It's a good story, but—"

"Do you believe you're a sinner?"

He shrugged. "Who knows what's sin?" He smiled. "I gotta go. Thanks for the break."

After that I often read to him other parts of the New Testament. I was never sure which he enjoyed: the Word or the opportunity to sit down.

One day he told me it was his last day on the route. "We're moving out to Orange County," he said. "Our first house."

"Jake! I'm glad for you, but I'm going to miss you. But —you still don't believe Jesus is the Messiah!"

He smiled kindly and shook his head. "He belongs to your religion. I have mine. Don't worry!"

"Jake, I'll make a bargain with you! If, after you move out there, someone else, a complete stranger, comes to you and tells you exactly what I've told you, will you believe that it is God, telling you to believe in Jesus?"

He squinted. "If somebody tries to convert me by saying the same things you have, I'd just about have to believe, wouldn't I?"

I'm sure I'll see Jake in heaven. God answered my prayer to have the courage to tell him of Jesus, and though Jake did not then accept Him, God is all *mercy*.

But because of his great love for us, God, who is rich in mercy, made us alive with Christ (Eph. 2:4).

Mind Sets

At a retreat, our son Ron dedicated his life to Christian service. He and I often talked about which Bible college would best suit his needs.

My husband never took part in these conversations, but he didn't seem opposed to the idea either. However, as graduation grew closer, he began to make remarks. "Ron, what a shame that anyone with an IQ like yours would waste it by becoming a preacher! What an engineer you'd make." Or, "You should look into electronics."

Ron always smiled apologetically, but he had higher orders to consider.

One evening Ron brought college brochures to the dinner table, so we could make definite arrangements. His dad seemed grim, ignoring the exciting talk. At last he said. "How do you plan to pay for your education?"

Ron looked stunned. Then he grinned a bit. "Well, if I go to Biola, I can work at the hamburger place."

"I suggest you get a better job than that," his dad said quietly. "I'm not going to help you go to this Bible college."

"What do you mean!" I exploded. "You said you'd pay half!"

He shrugged coldly. "I've decided I'll never help him become a preacher. If he decides to become an engineer or a lawyer or a doctor—I'll put a second mortgage on the house to pay his way." He stood up abruptly. "Excuse me."

Ron and I looked at each other. He gathered up the brochures. "Guess I'll throw these in the trash," he said.

"Let's pray!" I said, getting to my feet.

"Let's not," he said glumly. "We've been praying for dad for a year. He's getting worse. Anyway, maybe he's right."

"I know you don't believe that. Please, son, let's pray."

"It's not going to do any good, Mother."

I got on my knees and he flopped down beside me.

"I feel like the Lord is a million miles away," he said.

I felt the same way, but I said, "He's promised us that if we draw near to Him, He'll draw near to us."

We had prayed together so many times in the past, easily, naturally. But now we were both silent for a long time. Finally, I forced myself to begin:

"Lord, neither of us feels like praying. I feel mad and helpless and mixed up. I'm sure Ron feels the same way. He doesn't know whether You want him to go to a Bible college or not. And if You do, how can we pay for it? What shall we do, Lord? Please comfort us, and make a way."

Ron relaxed a little. When he stood up, he seemed bigger, taller. There was a hardness in his jawline that I hadn't seen before. "I *know* the Lord wants me at some Bible college. I've go to go."

He went to talk with his dad. When they came in, my husband put his arm around my shoulder.

Ron's going to Biola," he said. "I still think it's a waste of a mighty fine brain, but his mind is set."

"But you said you'd never—"

"I know, I know," my husband waved his hand and smiled. "I still wish he'd go into a profession where he could make some money. I thought I could force him. But he says he *has* to serve the Lord." He looked at Ron fuzzily. "What can I do? I love the kid."

Be strong and courageous. Do not be afraid or terrified because of them, for the Lord your God goes with you; he will never leave you nor forsake you (Deut. 31:6).

Green Lights

When Ron was in his first semester of college he called one evening. "I want you to meet someone," he said. Someone special. I'll bring her over Sunday."

"Good!" I said. "What would you like to have for dinner?"

"We won't be there for dinner, mother. I've been invited to her house."

I felt jealous. After I hung up I said to my husband, "We hardly ever get to see him! Why couldn't he bring her here for dinner?"

He looked at me sternly. "When are you going to let go of him? You and I were married when we were his age."

"Yet, but—" I went to our bedroom to lie down, but instead I pulled out an old scrapbook I started when Ron was born. I had recorded his weight each month, when he first drank orange juice, his first outing, when he could sit alone. The entries brought back his babyhood with bittersweet clarity. I could almost feel his cute body in my arms. Tears were falling when I turned to the last page, and there in my handwriting was a letter I had written to him. It told him how much I loved him and how glad I was to have a baby boy. I concluded the letter by writing, "And someday, when you find the right girl, I hope I will be courageous enough to let you go, with no strings attached."

I had only been twenty-one when I wrote that perceptive sentence. Surely I had as much sense now, didn't I? I cried all the harder. Quietly I slipped to my knees beside the bed.

"Oh Lord! Here I am again, still trying to run things. I'll bet Ron is really in love this time. Lord, I'm jealous and not ready to give him up. I know I'm being ugly. Please forgive me. If this is *the* girl, help me let go, and help me to love her."

After Sunday dinner I kept looking out the front window, watching for Ron's jalopy. At last he turned in the driveway and jerked to a stop. He leaped out and ran around to the other side to help a tall, lovely girl out of the car. She had shoulder-length, brown wavy hair, and from where I stood behind the drape, she looked like a model. I dashed to the couch and picked up the Sunday paper just before he banged open the door.

"Hiya, mother and dad! He looked ecstatic. I want you to meet Barbara!"

We had a good time that afternoon. Barbara was witty, but not a know-it-all. Pretty, but not phony. And she loved the Lord.

After they left, my husband said, "She reminds me of you. He'll marry this one."

"I know!" I said. "Isn't it wonderful?"

But the *most* wonderful thing was that the Lord had answered prayer. I *liked* her! She wasn't a threat to my happiness. She was going to be the whipped cream on my pecan pie!

For this reason a man will leave his father and mother and be united to his wife (Matt. 19:5–6).

The Disaster in My Mind

Ron and Barbara weren't formally engaged, but everyone knew they were serious. The church had even asked the two of them to lead junior church. The kids loved them, and it made me happy, not only because they were serving the Lord together, but because it meant Ron came home from campus on weekends.

One Saturday evening they went to a party, and although I trusted them, I felt uneasy about the situation. The boy who was giving the party was a new Christian. He was sincere in his belief in Christ, but he hadn't had much opportunity to grow. His parents were going to be out of town for the weekend, and he wanted to take advantage of having the house to himself.

"I'm sure his friends aren't Christians," Ron said, "but it will be a good opportunity for Barbara and me to witness and show him we care."

All evening I worried about the party. What were they doing? So many teenagers smoked pot, or worse. I was thankful our kids were Christians, and yet I knew even believers were tempted in such situations.

"If his faith is as strong as you think it is," my husband observed, with a trace of sarcasm, "he'll be all right."

With each passing hour I became more uneasy. *Why is it,* I wondered, *I am able to pray with such confidence about other people's problems, but right now, when my own children are the concern, I can't seem to get through to the Lord?* We finally went to bed, but after two hours of wide-eyed tossing I got up and went to the kitchen. In a few moments my husband joined me.

"What are you doing up?" he asked.

"It's two o'clock!" I said." Ron's not home!"

"So what?" my husband answered. "You and I used to stay out 'til three."

"Yes, but—Ron takes junior church seriously. It isn't like him to stay out this late on Saturday night." My stomach ached from being tense. "I *know* something is wrong."

My husband went to the living room and turned on the TV. I leaned against the refrigerator and prayed:

"Oh God! I'm so worried! You know where Ronnie is. Please, Lord, don't let him come to any harm. Oh dear God, please bring him home safely!"

I felt a little more at ease and decided to go into the living room. I saw a dark object on the carpet in front of the door. I leaned over to look at it. It was Ron's billfold!

"Look!" I screamed, and thrust it at my husband. "Oh I knew it! Somebody beat him up and then brought this to taunt us! Maybe he's lying dead somewhere! I'm going to call the police!" I started toward the phone, but my husband yanked open the front door. Ron's car was in the driveway, and he was slumped in the seat. *Is he unconscious?* I thought. When my husband pounded on the car window Ron sat up and smiled. He opened the door.

"Hi, dad. What time is it?"

"What are you doing out here?" my husband roared.

"Huh? Oh. I've been here since midnight, but I forgot my key. I didn't want to wake you, so I put my billfold through the mail slot, so if you did get up, you'd know I was okay."

The ordeal that I had made of this was over: my prayer had been answered even before I'd said the words.

Before they call I will answer; while they are still speaking I will hear (Isa. 65:24).

Minimum Payments

My husband was advancing in his company, and I was bringing home a modest salary from my job as church secretary, but our expenses climbed. With a daughter in high school and a son in college there never seemed to be any money left for special things. I'd always made most of Joan's clothes, but now she had to buy outfits I couldn't make, such as her Pep Club sweater and skirt. Besides, with my job, I didn't have time to sew, and I needed new clothes, too. Almost everyone we knew had charge accounts, so it was easy to start one of our own.

With my husband's permission, I opened a revolving account with one of the major department stores. What a wonderful feeling! Joan and I spent many Friday evenings and Saturday mornings browsing and charging. I felt rich.

I went along for a while, making minimum payments, but charging the maximum. We also decided to buy a new living room set on credit. With our house and car payments, our standard monthly bills, and two charge payments, we were in trouble. We began to juggle payments, and, of course, we began to receive past-due notices.

We talked about this with our neighbors one evening and one of them made an eye-opening remark: "The fine print on those revolving accounts says they can repossess everything you've bought, if you fail to make payment."

"You mean if I can't make this month's payment, they could come and take the sweater I bought for Joan six months ago?"

"Legally, yes."

I sat there numb, as I tried to recall all the things I had charged. What if they came and demanded all of it back?

After the neighbors went home I said, "I'm not buying another thing on that revolving account!"

"I wish you meant it," my husband sighed. "But what about Joan's graduation?"

My determination wavered. She would need a lot of things. Besides that, we were expecting relatives in the summer, and I wanted to get the house fixed up. How could I buy everything without resorting to credit?

I was hooked! Just like a junky. Hooked on credit.

I sat on our new couch and prayed:

"Dear Father, I remember the battle I had with cigarettes. You delivered me. Thank You again for that. Help me now to quit buying on credit, although I don't know how I can get through the next few months without it. You know there isn't enough cash for our needs."

"There is plenty for your needs. It is your covetousness that is the problem." I hadn't heard a voice, but I knew the Holy Spirit had contradicted me.

"Lord, forgive me," I answered, "for buying above our income. By Your power, this night, I *will* kick the charging habit."

I picked up my purse, took out the charge card, and cut it into small pieces. Each time I snipped, I prayed, "Help me, Lord."

It took over a year, but, by staying away from the stores and consciously thanking the Lord for everything we had, we finally saw a month where everything was paid off, and we opened a savings account!

The Lord had given us another victory!

Let no debt remain outstanding, except the continuing debt to love one another (Rom. 13:8).

The Satin Finish

"Can you use this piece of material?" my neighbor asked, handing me four and one half yards of bright green satin. "I've had it for three years, but I can't seem to find the right pattern for it."

"Oh! It's gorgeous!" I said as I carressed the shimmery material between my fingers.

At home, Joanie sniffed disdainfully. "What can you do with *that*?"

"I'm sure I'll find the right one," I said, riffling through patterns. "I really need a new dress."

"But mother! That material should be used for an evening gown. Or a dinner dress!"

"Doesn't have to be." I said. "How about this?" I held up a pattern for a two-piece suit.

She looked at the ceiling and groaned. "Why don't you wait and get the right pattern?"

"If I get started now" I said, "I'll have a new dress to wear Sunday." Without asking for any more of her advice, I put the pattern box away and began to smooth out the tissue pattern pieces.

"You're starting it tonight?" Joan asked.

Quickly I pinned the paper to the fabric.

"Aren't you even going to press the material? she exclaimed.

Everyone was in bed when I was ready for the first fitting. Eagerly, I put on the skirt and coat and stood in front of the hall mirror. Something was wrong at the shoulders.

59

"Rats," I mumbled to myself. "I should have taken time to baste it. Now I'll have to rip out those seams."

But at midnight I breathed a sigh of relief. The machine work was done. The next night I could scarcely wait to get started on the hand work.

"Soon as I'm through with my shower, I'll pin the hem for you, Mother," Joan called.

But I didn't want to wait.

"Oh Mother!" Joan cried when she saw the skirt. "It sags in the back, and it's too short in front." It took another hour to take it out and put it in again.

I set up the ironing board to press the finished garment. (None of that pressing-seams-as-you-go for me). I put the iron on "steam," but none came out. I jiggled it, and pushed the button several times. Suddenly it spat a stream of dirty water right on the front of the skirt! I tried to sponge it away. I washed the whole skirt, but even after it was dry, the sediment left its mark. The suit was *ruined*.

All my frantic sewing had been for nothing. I began to cry, and then complained to the Lord:

"Lord! Why did you allow this to happen? You *know* I wear the same things over and over. You know I needed that dress! What did I do wrong? Why are you punishing me?"

While the tears were still flowing, He seemed to whisper:

"My daughter, I'm not punishing you. I love you. I'm simply teaching you part of the fruit of the Spirit. You need *patience* more than you need a dress."

Only later, did I realize He was not only trying to teach me patience, He was also protecting me from looking ridiculous or cheap in a tight, satin dress.

The end of a matter is better than its beginning, and patience is better than pride (Eccl. 7:8).

A Change of Heart

My husband decided to go into business for himself. And I was proud of him. But my heart sank when he said, "I want you to be my bookkeeper and secretary."

The thought of giving up my position as pastor's secretary shocked me. I loved my job! I didn't want to leave it.

He went on: "Let's jump in the car and see the building."

My heart dropped even lower when he stopped in front of a run-down building, set in a yard of waist-high weeds. Inside, it reeked of old oil and filth. A rat scurried through the former tenant's rubbish.

"I'll partition off this one big room," he said, his eyes sparkling. "Of course, it will look better when it's clean and painted."

How horrid, I moaned to myself. *Stuck away in this rat-hole all day. I can't stand it.*

My husband looked at me, and I could see his excitement drain away and anger take its place. He could see my tears near the brimming point.

"Well, bro-o-*ther!*" he exploded. "You're great encouragement!" He spun away from me. "Forget it! I'll get someone else."

"No! Wait!" I reached out for him. "It's—just—I guess I didn't realize you would need someone in the office. You—you know I want to help you." He turned slightly and the hurt on his face tore at my heart. "Let's talk about it some more." I coaxed. "Over coffee?"

From the car I watched him loop a rusty chain through

61

the yard gate. I shook my head. This had to be the most desolate time in my life.

"Oh God!" I prayed silently. "You know how I love the work at church, and I don't want to work here! But Lord, I know my place is with my husband. So *please,* this minute, give me Your power to act as if I were enthusiastic and to be the helper he needs." There was a painful lump in my throat, and my eyes burned with unshed tears. "Just get me through this, Lord."

As my husband got in the car, I thought, *This yard wouldn't look too bad if all the weeds were gone and we had planted a few shrubs and flowers.*

"There's a shopping center less than a block away," my husband said in a flat voice.

In a moment I saw a big food market, a variety store, several small shops, and a discount department store. *I could even do some shopping on the noon hour,* I thought.

As we drank our coffee the Lord showed me several more advantages to the new situation: no more evening phone calls about church matters, no traffic to fight, and I could wear more casual clothes!

A flame of enthusiasm flared inside me. I looked at my husband, still tight-lipped. And wasn't it wonderful he wanted me instead of some young secretary!

"I guess I'm going to enroll in night school," I said. "I know shorthand and typing but not bookkeeping."

We both smiled shyly, and I reached for his hand. I realized then the Lord had not only given me power to "put on a happy face," but He had actually exchanged my despair for genuine enthusiasm.

Now to him who is able to do immeasurably more than all we ask or imagine, according to his power that is at work within us, to him be glory (Eph. 3:20–21).

A Battle Call

Our contracting business was located in an industrial part of the city. Our property was fenced, and the only way to get in or out was through the gate. Early one morning I was in the office alone, completely absorbed in book-keeping. No one came to our office this early, so I was startled when the door opened. A tall, handsome young man had come in without knocking.

"Can I use your phone?" he asked. "I work next door in the boat yard, and I want to call my boss to see why he hasn't showed up."

I nodded and motioned to the phone on my desk. But I asked myself, *how did he get in?* My husband had locked the gate. I pushed the telephone over to the edge of my desk for the man's convenience. After dialing, he edged around slowly, until he was only inches from me. I wasn't exactly afraid, but I was very uncomfortable.

"How did you get in?" I asked, while he waited for the call to go through.

"Climbed over, he said, looking smug. His eyes bored into mine until I looked away. I crossed over to my hus-band's desk and pretended to look at papers. I froze when I heard him put the telephone in its cradle. I turned slightly to look at him and saw him start toward me.

I was this man's quarry! No one could hear me if I screamed. He was big, young, and strong. With a gasp, I darted behind the drawing board, then back to my desk, with him leaping at me. He grabbed my arm and pulled me to his chest. I fought with all my strength, but he kissed me on the mouth. Sickened, I jerked away, and I don't know if I cried it out loud, or only to myself, but I prayed!

"Jesus! Save me!"

What power there is in the name of Jesus! I was filled with His power and indignation. I looked at the man with all the scorn and disgust possible. "You ought to be ashamed!" I grated through my teeth. "Haven't you ever heard of *Jesus*?"

He looked shocked.

I pressed my advantage. "What's the matter with you anyway? Are you sick? I'm old enough to be your mother. I'm a Christian! Do you know what that means?"

His eyes were as round as a little boy's and I knew the Lord had given me the victory. Without taking my eyes off his face I picked up my Bible and waved it in the air. He began to back away toward the door.

"Lady, I don't know what came over me. I'm sorry—honest. Are you—please—don't tell my boss!"

"I don't know about that," I said imperiously. "But I will certainly tell my husband! Now wait a minute." I began to dig through some tracts in the desk drawer. "Don't go until I give you these." I handed him several tracts. "Read these," I commanded, "and if you want to learn more about Jesus Christ, I'll be glad to talk to you, providing my husband is present. Otherwise, don't ever come into this office again."

I never saw him again. But once more the Lord proved He is mighty, that He hears us, and that He fights our battles for us.

I called on your name, O LORD. . . . You heard my plea. . . . You came near when I called you (Lam. 3:55–57).

What Can I Say?

Although I was working for my husband full time, I agreed to decorate our church's fellowship hall for the mother-daughter banquet.

The theme was "Far Above Rubies," a biblical phrase describing women. "Far above" made me think of heaven. I could use angel hair for clouds; red carnations for floral centerpieces; and I could spray paint stones red and roll them in red glitter to simulate rubies!

At the office I could hardly wait to gather the stones from our gravel yard and start painting them. I had them all spread out on newspaper in the center of the floor, spraying up a red storm, when my husband came in, accompanied by a stranger. I jumped up guiltily.

"I didn't expect you back so soon," I murmured. "I'm in charge of table decorations for a mother and daughter banquet," I explained to the man. With red fingers I pointed at the floor. "These are rubies," I giggled.

My husband looked as though I'd announced we had cockroaches. I tried to move the newspapers and the rocks rolled, like a pinball machine out of control.

After the man left I knew I was going to be reprimanded and I deserved it. Or did I? After all, wasn't the Lord's work supposed to come first? I came to work early and stayed late. When did I have time for *His* projects?

"Do you know who that man was?" my husband shouted. "Chief engineer for Royal Engineering!" He jammed his hands into his pockets. "Rocks all over the floor! Don't you care anything about our reputation? The church! That's all you care about!"

"Maybe you'd do better if you cared more about the church!" I retorted. "You claim to be a Christian, but you don't go to church or read the Bible!" His mouth opened, and I rushed on. "No wonder you aren't getting the jobs you bid on! The Lord is punishing you!" I gathered up the rocks and, without looking back, I banged out the door.

At home the grimness of the situation began to sink in. What *had* I done?

"Oh, Lord!" I cried. "I'm so awful. I'm sorry I yelled at him. But Lord, why doesn't he believe, like I do? He's heard the gospel over and over. Lord, what else can I *say?*"

"That's the problem," the Spirit seemed to answer. "You *say* too much."

"But Lord, how is he—"

I stopped, as still as a statue. I had prayed for the Lord to tell me what to say, but the Lord answered, *"Be Quiet."*

When my husband came home, he was belligerent. "I'm going to bed," he growled.

But I had already promised the Lord, by His power, I would *Never* again quote Scripture at him, or tell him he ought to go to church. All I said was, "I want to apologize for the mess in the office, and for yelling at you."

The next day he insisted I take the rocks to work; he sprayed them and I rolled them in glitter. We were as polite as strangers to each other, and, although he probably thought I was still angry, I tried to show him with love and smiles that my quietness was not "irateness."

Being quiet is still not one of my virtues—but the Lord and I are working on it.

Wives, in the same way be submissive to your husbands so that, if any of them do not believe the word, they may be won over without talk by the behavior of their wives (1 Peter 3:1).

Red-letter Lesson

After being in business for himself about five years, my husband went back to his former position in an oil company. Soon I needed something to occupy my time. So I talked my husband into allowing me to start a small Christian book store, the Antioch Book and Gift Shop. At first I thought the only requisites to being a successful Christian bookstore owner were to love Jesus, love people, and love to read. What a lot the Lord had to teach me!

Finally, I learned to commit each new day to him, especially in the areas of *relying* on His wisdom, (praying, "Lord, I need you"), *trusting* His love, ("Lord, I'm not afraid") and *submitting* to His decisions, ("Lord, I give in"). I learned that *if* I remembered to commit these three areas to him, my life was peaceful and joyful no matter how hectic or how disappointing the day might be. But the hardest of these to put into practice was *submitting*.

One evening an elegant-looking middle-aged woman came into the shop, just as I was closing. I groaned. I had to get home, make dinner, and do the dishes. She looked at gifts up front, then slowly ambled back to the counter.

"Yes?" I said, shaking my keys.

"I'm looking for . . . I think it is the Scofield Bible." I sighed and went to the Bible counter. A Scofield sale was worth staying open a couple of minutes, but I surely hoped she would buy it and leave before someone else came in.

I put several Scofields in various leathers and sizes out on the counter. She methodically picked up each one, examined it slowly, and put it back in its box. I kept looking up at the clock and drumming my fingers.

"I am looking for a red-letter edition," she said.

"Scofield doesn't come in red letter," I said irritably. I looked at the ceiling and prayed silently:

"Lord! Help this woman make up her mind and get out of here. You know I'm tired."

I began to close the boxes so she would get the idea. But the Holy Spirit gave me a good, hard punch. He seemed to say, "Do you remember it was just this morning you asked Me to use you in this business? You *submitted* yourself to Me. Is this submission?"

I bit my lip and thought, *Sorry, Lord.*

A great surge of strength flowed into my body. I wasn't a bit tired! Genuine kindness reached out to this woman. What was half an hour in the light of eternity?

I practically jumped to get more Bibles to show her.

"Cambridge and Harper have beautiful red letter Bibles," I said.

"I must have misunderstood the pastor. You see, I have just accepted Jesus Christ as my Savior, and I want to read all His words!" She smiled at me. "The pastor said you would help me find the right Bible!"

I was filled with pain and regret. Why hadn't I been sweet to my new sister from the moment she entered the store? I thought of my selfish prayer a few minutes before and was glad the Lord hadn't granted that petition.

Submitting to the Lord is a hard thing to do, but I've learned it's the key to peace and joy.

Moreover, we have all had human fathers who disciplined us and we respected them for it. How much more should we submit to the Father of our spirits and live! (Heb. 12:9).

The Turned Table

As owner and manager of a Christian bookstore, I began to receive quite a few calls for Christian records and tapes. I always referrred these requests to Pete, a charming Jewish man who owned the record store in our shopping center.

"He doesn't carry much in the way of Christian music," one customer told me. "A few of Kate Smith's and Tennessee Ernie Ford's old standbys, but nothing new."

"But he does order for you, doesn't he?"

"He's not eager," my customer sniffed. "Says none of his suppliers carry what we want."

I thought about it, read all I could find in the catalogues, then decided I would add a small record section. Pete came in one day and I told him about my decision.

Like a bull he charged up to the glass counter and pounded on it with a heavy fist. "You can't sell records!" he roared. His dark eyes popped wide open.

"Wait a minute, Pete. We won't be in competition. I just want to stock a few Christian records."

"You're not stocking *any* records!" He turned his back and began to stride toward the door. "Look at your lease!" he called over his shoulder, as he butted out. The little brass bell banged hard against the plate glass door. I was too stunned to think clearly for a while. Then I went to the back room and dug out the lease. The "legalese" was hard to understand, but I found the clause that said I could not stock anything found in the other stores in the center, without their permission. So. Pete was right. I couldn't stock records—unless he said I could.

Right then I kneeled on the cold tile beside the beat-up desk and prayed:

"Dear Lord, maybe I'm not supposed to carry Christian records. But every other Christian bookstore has them. If it's Your will for me to sell them, then You will have to soften Pete's heart. Only You can change his mind."

Later on in the day I felt compelled to talk to Pete. I didn't want to face him, but I couldn't shake the urge. I locked up my store and ran down to the record shop.

"Hi, Pete." I grinned at him. "I found the clause—and you're right. I'm sorry. So, from now on, I'll tell all my customers that you will order for them, okay?"

He barely shrugged, but there was a hint of softness in his eyes.

Three days later he came in the store. "Can you use some more greeting cards? he asked.

"How come?" I asked, suspiciously.

"Before you opened up, I stocked a few cards. But no-body buys 'em. I need the space. You can have what's left."

"Oh, Pete! Thank you!"

He waved away my thanks. "About those religious records—actually, they're a real pain. Special orders waste my time. So, far as I'm concerned, you can stock them."

"Oh thank you, Pete. That's wonder—"

"But mind you!" He raised his finger threateningly. "No rock 'n roll!"

How great our Lord is. He not only changed Pete's mind, but the greeting cards he gave me totaled about two hundred dollars—wholesale!

This is what the LORD says to you: "Do not be afraid or discouraged.... For the battle is not yours, but God's" (2 Chron. 20:15).

Out of Control

"Oh," I moaned one night after dinner, "that pain under my left shoulder blade is getting worse."

"Make an appointment with the doctor," my husband ordered. "I'll be glad when the new owners can take over—you're overworked."

I didn't want to see the doctor, but I had to admit something was wrong. "Okay," I said. "I'll find time tomorrow."

Idly, I massaged the back of my neck and scalp. Suddenly, my fingertips hit an area behind my right ear that felt blank—bare. With mounting horror, I rushed to the bathroom and snatched up the hand mirror. I saw a *bald* spot about the size of a silver dollar. Heartsick and scared, the night seemed endless. As soon as he would see me, I hurried to the doctor.

When he saw the bald spot, he let out his breath. He leaned back and looked at me through bifocals.

"What are you worrying about?" he asked.

He'd been our doctor for years. Periodically, I'd witnessed to him about the peace and rest I had as a Christian, so it was an affront for him to ask me this.

"I'm not worrying," I said indignantly.

"You may not think so, but you are. That pain in your back is the start of an ulcer, and you may lose all your hair if you don't get relief from whatever is bothering you."

When I got on the freeway I still felt indignant. Me worry? Didn't I get up early so I could have personal devotions? Didn't I pray? I put on the blinker and edged out into traffic.

71

As the car accelerated, so did my heart, and I felt that sinking sensation in my stomach that was becoming so familiar. Suddenly, I was surrounded by too many cars, and I was going too fast. I jammed on the brakes to keep from smashing into the car ahead. I was sweaty and tremulous. I felt confused—would my exit never come?

At home I sank down on the couch and burst into tears. I hugged a pillow in an effort to quit shaking. I felt as though I might start screaming uncontrollably. I *was* worrying. My mind was always on the problems of managing the book store. I thought I was trusting the Lord, but I could read a whole chapter of the Bible and not know what I had read. I could pray up a storm, and still be thinking about the store. Devotions had become a form, something to whip through before rushing to work. Where was God?

I guess I'd left Him out. I fell to my knees:

"Dear Lord, forgive me for not casting all this work on You. What a poor testimony I've been—especially to the doctor. He knows I've been worrying instead of resting. From this moment, Lord, I give You all my worries—the bald spot, the pain, the responsibility of ordering, training, the customers, everything. I can't do it without You."

Later that evening the pain disappeared—forever! It was a year before my bald spot grew back in, but that day my hair quit falling out.

Did I become lazy and useless in the remaining weeks at the store? No, I think I was more efficient than ever. I just got back to concentrating on each morning's Bible study and consciously, deliberately, committing every detail of each day to the Lord.

Therefore do not worry about tomorrow, for tomorrow will worry about itself (Matt. 6:34).

When the Heat Is On

Several months after I was through working at the bookstore mother and I went out of town to visit friends. I decided to return by a more scenic route, one that led up over the foothills. As we started down the steep, two-lane highway, I glanced over at mother. She was eighty-five and suffered with arteriosclerosis, which she called "heart-trouble." It was a hot day, and I could see she was starting to have one of her "spells." I began to look for a place where I could pull over alongside the narrow road.

"Don't worry about me," she said, as she put a tiny white pill under her tongue. "I'm just tired—and it's so hot." I put the air conditioner on "maximum," but it didn't cool the car very fast.

A few minutes later mother looked better, but I began having trouble steering. "What's the matter with this dumb thing?" I mumbled as I swerved over the yellow line. I fought my way around two more curves before it dawned on me: *I have a flat tire!* Now I *had* to find a place to stop.

I found a long, wide shoulder just around the next curve. When I got out of the car and walked back, the right rear tire was a sad sight, spread out in the hot gravel like a blob of melted tar.

Tension boiled up. Now what? I didn't know if I could change a tire or not. But I had learned not to worry. Pray!

"Oh God, You're the help of the helpless—and that's me. I don't know anything about changing tires. And You know all about mother and this heat. Somehow, Lord, get this problem solved. Thank You."

Calmness bathed my mind and body. I was relaxed, almost unconcerned as I opened the trunk. We were on a remote mountain road, with no telephone for miles. In this heat, mother could have a stroke any minute. I didn't even have any water for her to drink. But I had the Lord. He had taken me through ulcers. He would see us through this problem.

In the trunk, I saw a beach towel. I shook the sand out of it and went around to mother's side of the car.

"Honey, we've got a flat tire," I told her. She looked frightened. "Now, now, don't worry! Let's put this towel up in the window to keep the sun off of you, and we'll open my door—" My genuine calmness soothed her, and, wonder of wonders, a breeze began to riffle the towel. I squeezed her hand, then went back to the trunk. Just as I put the jack on the ground, loud air brakes "whooshed" right behind me. I whirled around to face the front end of a massive truck.

"Looks like you've got trouble," the slender driver said as he took the jack handle out of my hand. Within minutes he'd changed the tire.

He wouldn't take any money, and I forgot to read the company name on the truck. And what was a big semi doing on that mountain road anyway?

Thank You, Lord!

Do not be anxious about anything, but in everything, by prayer and petition, with thanksgiving, present your requests to God. And the peace of God, which transcends all understanding, will guard your hearts and your minds in Christ Jesus (Phil. 4:6–7).

The Mailman Cometh

One day I got an idea for a salvation tract, sat down at the typewriter, wrote it, and then mailed it to a publisher. In about three weeks I received a small check. They were going to publish it! I was a writer! The idea of becoming a *writer* took possession of me. At the library I checked out every book I could find on the craft, and everything I read encouraged and excited me. I wrote a travel piece on our vacation trip. I wrote a children's story about a boy and his dog, complete with drawings! I wrote a "how-to" piece on being a welcome guest. I spent hours at the typewriter, and I spent more money on postage in three months than I had in three years. I thought of myself as "the writer in the family," and I dominated the conversation with "writing talk." I was a real bore. Besides that, I passed out hundreds of *my* tract. Of course I wanted people to be saved, but I wonder: Was that my motive, or did I just want people to know I was a writer?

One by one, the stamped, self-addressed, brown envelopes came back home, dragging their tales inside them. With every rejected manuscript I became more deflated, until at last I felt like an old inner tube.

One day, after the mailman brought a reject instead of a check, I plopped down at the kitchen table. I blurted out at God:

"What's the matter with these dumb publishers? Don't they know good material when they see it?"

The Spirit reprimanded me immediately, but I was too

proud and hurt to say I was sorry. All dreams of becoming a famous writer were fading. Even though I'd sold one tract and thought I had talent, I must have been mistaken. I tried not to cry, but my throat hurt as if I had tonsillitis, and the tears came anyway. I jumped up and tossed the brown envelope in the trash. I was a failure. A big zero. Staring out the kitchen window, I prayed:

"Lord, what's wrong with my writing? I thought You wanted me to write, but nothing sells. What's wrong? I don't have the heart to try again. Please, comfort me, encourage me."

I poured a cup of coffee and sat back down. For the first time, I glanced at a brochure the mailman had delivered. It listed courses offered through adult education. Without interest, I opened it. The words *creative writing* leaped out at me! A writing class was scheduled every Thursday morning at 9:00. This was the answer! The dear Lord *was* encouraging me. He wanted me to keep on, but I needed to learn some things. I'd been overconfident, and yes, even conceited. I enrolled for the coming semester, and, humbly, I learned that one published piece does not a writer make.

Do not be proud. . . . Do not be conceited (Rom. 12:16).

He Is Life!

At last I was a grandmother! Holding Laurie, I knew that nothing had ever thrilled me more. What a dollie! How intelligent! Ooooh! I just wanted to *squeeze* her! Caring for her was a privilege.

One night mother and I went to Ron and Barbara's house to take care of Laurie while they went to a church function. Before we'd had nearly enough loving and cuddling, it was time for them to come home. Naturally Laurie must be clean, dry, and ready for bed when mommy came in, so I took her to the nursery and put her on top of the bathinette to change her.

"Getchoo!" I cooed to her. "You darling, pink thing! Look how big she is, mother!"

Mother tried to capture a foot to kiss. "She is getting big—of course, she's three months old."

With my hand firmly on Laurie's tummy I said, "Hand me a diaper, will you, mother?"

"Sure—where are they?"

"Over there—see? On that chest."

But she couldn't see them.

"That's okay, mother. I'll get one."

I crossed the space in one quick step, but in that second, when my back was turned, our darling baby girl flipped off the table. It was the most horrible thud I've ever heard. There she lay, on the hardwood floor, still as death, unconscious.

I screamed and scooped her up in my arms. Her face,

which had been pink and laughing a moment before, was now white as marble. As I watched, her eyelids turned blue.

"Oh, God!" I cried out in agony. "*Jesus*! Don't let this baby die!"

Like a person in a trance, I stood there, horrified, helpless, with Laurie in my arms.

Mother grabbed her from me.

Calmly, she pinched Laurie's pug nose between her fingers and put her wrinkled lips on the baby's mouth; she blew gently, once, twice, three times.

With a tiny catch in her throat, our baby began to breathe again. Her eyelids fluttered, and she let out a howl of indignation!

Over the telephone the doctor told Barbara to keep her awake for an hour and to call him again if she didn't seem normal. But she was all right, thank God.

Some people said she'd probably only had the wind knocked out of her. But *I* was there; she was as good as dead. When I called out to the all-powerful name of Jesus, He acted through my mother, who, just the week before, had read an article on how to give mouth-to-mouth resuscitation.

He knows what we need even before we ask!

[Jesus] said, "My child, get up!" Her spirit returned, and at once she stood up (Luke 8:54–55).

Show Me!

"It's called the Dead Sea," the Sunday school teacher explained, "because the fresh water that flows into it, can't flow out of it. Because the sea has no outlets, minerals have accumulated until the salt concentration is four times greater than that of the ocean. Nothing can live in it, and so it's practically useless." He paused and seemed to look right at me. "I wonder, are some of us Dead Sea Christians, always taking in and never giving out?"

His words stung, because, although I'd been a member for a long time, I wasn't currently active in any kind of church-related service. I was self-employed as a writer; that was my contribution to the work of the kingdom.

But I offered to help, I thought, *and the Lord definitely told me to write, Writing takes a lot of time.*

"Yes," agreed my conscience, "but how about people who have eight-hour-a-day jobs and still teach Sunday school or work in junior church?" I kept arguing with myself during church service.

But if I take a Sunday school class, think how much preparation it requires! There isn't just the lesson, there are house calls, visual aids—I wouldn't have much time for writing.

"Granted," my other self agreed. "But how about the choir?"

My voice isn't very good, I answered.

"Not terrific, but you can read music. Use it or lose it."

During the invitation hymn I prayed:

"Lord Jesus, am I a Dead Sea Christian? I sincerely want to do what You want me to do. I know You want me to write, but do You want me in the choir? If You do, then make someone ask me."

The hymn books were barely in the racks when I felt a tap on my shoulder. I turned around to greet one of the choir members. She'd just returned from vacation and had enjoyed a Sunday "off," sitting in the congregation.

"You have a good alto voice," she said. "Why don't you join the choir?"

Coincidence? No! It was the Lord communicating His desire. I was at choir practice Wednesday night, and the song in my heart was much more beautiful than the song from my voice.

Let the desert and its towns raise their voices.... Let the people ... sing for joy (Isa. 42:11).

Waiting for Weight

Even in her late thirties my sister's shape and features —wide-set bluish green eyes, copper-colored hair, and creamy skin—made men's heads turn and women— including me—jealous.

After we were converted, however, my sister's attitude toward herself changed. She saw how proud she'd been and sincerely wanted to die to self, following Paul's example: "I have been crucified with Christ and I no longer live, but Christ lives in me" (Gal. 2:20). She squelched any desire to be glamorous. She gave away her sparkling party dresses and her jewelry, and she quit wearing make-up.

"And I'm not going to wear slacks, either," she announced. "They're too revealing. I don't want people to look at my shape. I want them to see Christ in me."

Never having had a beautiful figure, I couldn't quite see her point. I continued to wear pants, even though she frowned on it.

Before this, she'd always been on some kind of a diet, but now she began to *enjoy* her meals. One day I gently pointed out she was becoming a little too curvy.

"Oh, foo," she said and waved her hand. "Dieting is vanity. I try not to think of *self* at all."

For the next several years, in spite of mild hints from all her family, she continued to gain weight. She finally admitted she was too heavy, but said: "I just want to serve the Lord. He doesn't care if I'm glamorous. He looks on the heart."

Her attitude disturbed all of us. Besides, she was having physical problems—swollen joints, shortness of breath, and borderline diabetes. Periodically, she tried to cut down, but her "won't power" only lasted a few days at a time.

One day my mother, my niece, and I agreed to pray for her, that she would go on a diet that would work. We continued to pray for her for several weeks, and I'm sure she was also praying, because one happy day she told us that her eating was as much self-indulgence as her vanity had been, and that she had joined "Weight Watchers"! In a year she was her former slender, healthy, lovely self.

And then, we stopped praying.

In another year she had regained almost all her weight.

"I can't bear to go on a diet again!" she stormed. "If you don't love me as I am, then it's too bad. And that's final."

We all got back on our knees. I put my prayer on a card, so I'd be reminded to pray daily:

"Give sis the desire to lose weight again—for Your glory and for her health's sake."

It took awhile, but gradually, the desire to be a good testimony to the Lord and to look her best for her husband took hold of her, and once again she began to count calories.

That was three years ago, and I'm fully convinced that if we had not quit praying for her, she would not have had to go through the ordeal of another diet. Forgive us, Lord, for not praying.

Today, my sis weighs what she did when she was young. She is vibrant, youthful, and useful. And we've learned that we need to pray for some victories *continually,* even after the Lord has won the first battle.

Be alert, and always keep on praying for all the saints (Eph. 6:18).

Bygones

One morning I awoke with the heavy feeling something was wrong. I looked at the clock. 8:15! Where was my husband? Why hadn't the alarm gone off? I sat up and listened. There were no sounds anywhere in the house. Evidently, he'd turned off the alarm and gone to work. That meant he was still angry. I got out of bed and slowly put on my robe. But who could blame him after the way I'd hurt him last night?

We had quarreled. I couldn't even remember what started it, but it was one of those quarrels where we both outdid the other in saying unkind things. I finally went too far and made a nasty remark about the past. I knew at the time it hurt him, but he had hurt me, too! I had marched out of the living room, so he couldn't retaliate, and got ready for bed! By the time I pulled the covers up I felt miserable. The Spirit was telling me not to let the sun go down while I was still angry, but I stubbornly stayed where I was. Later, when I felt my husband get in bed, I was tempted to reach out and tell him I was sorry. But I was *always* the one to say I was sorry. This time I was not going to give in. After a long time we both went to sleep.

I shivered in my robe. He hadn't turned up the furnace or even made coffee. When I looked out the kitchen window the empty garage stared at me accusingly. I dialed his office.

"Please forgive me," I heard myself saying. "That remark was unfair."

"Forget it," he said. "I can't talk now." He hung up.

All morning, as I did housework, I tried to forget it, but I couldn't. My guilt oppressed me. Wouldn't I ever learn to have a gentle and quiet spirit? At last I went to the Lord, broken and sad.

"Dear heavenly Father, please forgive me for being cruel and unfair. My tongue is not tamed. And I resisted You, when You wanted me to make things right last night. Lord, it seems the older I get, the more sinful I am. I ask You to forgive once again."

Immediately His golden presence engulfed me, loving me, lifting me. Scripture verses came to mind to show me that He not only forgives confessed sin, but He forgets. Hallelujah!

The phone rang.

"Sorry to cut you off awhile ago," my husband said. "I had a salesman in the office. But I want you to know everything is okay. And I let you sleep this morning because you needed it. You've been working too hard."

Thank You Lord for *Today. Yesterday* is past.

I, even I, am he who blots out your transgressions, for my own sake, and remembers your sins no more (Isa. 43:25).

Mirror, Mirror, on the Wall

One Saturday, as I was cleaning house, I took a mirror off the wall and placed it face up on the coffee table so I could polish it better. As I looked into the mirror, I saw all the flesh on my face sag with the weight of years. Deep circles darkened my eye sockets; the lines around my mouth turned down; my skin looked dry, and the flesh on my neck looked like discarded pantyhose.

In my head, I knew outward appearance wasn't important, but my ego didn't agree. It *hurt* to get old. Oh, if only I could be young again! I pulled up the skin in front of my ears and was amazed at the difference. Maybe I could wear my hair pulled tight—or better, get a face lift!

That evening, every beautiful young girl on television was like a knife cutting my heart. Wasn't it just a couple of years ago some fellows in a car had whistled at *me*? That night in bed I cried for my past youth, with its firm flesh and peach-colored skin.

The next morning I didn't feel any better. In fact, my knee joints hurt. I wasn't getting old; I *was* old!

"I wish you'd tell me what's wrong," my husband said. "Have I offended you?"

"I'm just old," I said, "and ugly."

"Nobody's getting younger, you know. Look at the creases in my face."

"But it's different for a woman!" I said, and I rushed to the bathroom and cried some more. After some time, I kneeled beside the bathtub. The enamel felt cold on my arms, and the dripping faucet underscored my heartache:

"Lord Jesus, I'm miserable. I know I'm being self-centered again, but I thought I would grow old gracefully. Nobody told me it would hurt so much! Help me, Father, to accept old age as part of Your perfect plan for my life. Please, right now, replace this sadness with joy."

I knew from past experience that He would answer. And as a token of my faith, I washed my face and put on fresh lipstick. Already some long-forgotten Bible verses were filtering through to my mind. Paul said we should fix our eyes, not on what is seen, but, on what is unseen. Abraham and Sarah were both old, in their nineties, before they had Isaac. Moses was eighty-something when he started trying to persuade Pharaoh to let the people go. And Elizabeth and Zechariah were "well along in years" when they had John. These people had contributed most during their later years.

My sadness was evaporating, and, although I didn't exactly feel like laughing, a slow joy was building.

"There's my beautiful wife," my husband said when I went back to the living room.

"Now don't make fun of me," I said.

"I'm not making fun of you. Sure, there are thousands of beautiful young women, but I love *you*. You see thousands of handsome men, don't you? Does that mean you don't love me?"

I began to smile. Oh, thank You, Lord. Of course the world was full of handsome young men—but I only wanted my husband.

"Anyway," he added tenderly, "I think your wrinkles are cute."

Even to your old age and gray hairs I am he, I am he who will sustain you. I have made you and I will carry you; I will sustain you and I will rescue you (Isa. 46:4).

A Time for Us?

What a relief—moving to a condominium. No more worry about maintenance, painting, or roofing. Now we would have time!

"Let's not get acquainted with our neighbors," I suggested. "At least for a while. We'll just lay around and get tanned and read and relax."

"And not get involved," my husband agreed.

We enjoyed our privacy for about six months, when one night we were awakened by screaming and angry, profane shouts. The people next door were having a terrible fight. We heard thuds along with the screams.

"Our neighbors sure need the Lord," I said.

Soon another neighbor, a chic woman in her sixties, knocked on our door. "I hate to bother you," she began, "but I've locked my keys in my car!"

While my husband manipulated a wire through the rubber around the window, I learned her husband had deserted her a long time ago. She was looking forward to retirement. "If I make it," she sighed. "I'm so tired, and it's not easy when you're alone."

Poor, dear, lady. She also needed the Lord.

That Sunday afternoon we went outside to play a game of Yard Darts. It wasn't long before we had an audience of our boys. Their mother was divorced. No, they didn't go to church. I heard my husband offer to help fix one of the boys' bikes. "It's rough when there's no dad around," he whispered to me.

The next Saturday morning I was in our carport when a tall young man zoomed up on a skate board. "Hi! My name's Ben! I live in the condo behind you." Ben was also divorced and unbearably lonely. "Sure I'll go to church with you," he said. "Sometime—"

There were almost three hundred units in our association. Was the Lord trying to tell us something? We wanted to rest, the last thing we wanted was to get involved, and yet . . .

"I've been thinking the same thing," my husband said, when I told him my thoughts. "I think we'd better rededicate our lives to the Lord and be willing to be used as He directs."

We both knelt by the couch and he led in prayer:

"Lord Jesus, forgive us for being selfish and wanting to live just for ourselves. Lord, we know You died for each and every person in this association, so we give ourselves back to you. Use us for Your glory."

A change came over us. We pulled back our drapes, and, weather permitting, left our front door open. We invited friendship.

At the next association meeting my husband was elected vice president, and later president. He didn't want either job. But we both know the Lord put him there. I now write the newsletter, and I've already put in a few spiritual "blurbs." Ben has gone to church three times and calls our church his. One man, anticipating heart surgery, asked us to pray for him. It's not much, but it's a start.

"Thank You Lord, for using us, for showing us the needs in our own "back yard" and forgive our selfishness. And thank You, Lord, for teaching us to pray.

Therefore, I urge you, brothers, in view of God's mercy, to offer your bodies as living sacrifices, holy and pleasing to God—which is your spiritual worship (Rom. 12:1).